Rookie
Read-About Science®

Let's Visit
Some Islands

By Allan Fowler

Consultants

Linda Cornwell, Learning Resource Consultant,
Indiana Department of Education

Sharyn Fenwick, Elementary Science/Math Specialist,
Gustavus Adolphus College, St. Peter, Minnesota

Children's Press®
A Division of Grolier Publishing
New York   London   Hong Kong   Sydney
Danbury, Connecticut

Visit Children's Press® on the Internet at:
http://publishing.grolier.com

Designer: Herman Adler Design Group

Library of Congress Cataloging-in-Publication Data

Fowler, Allan.
    Let's visit some islands / by Allan Fowler.
        p. cm. – (Rookie read-about science)
    Includes index.
    Summary: Explains the difference between islands and continents,
tells how they were formed, and points out that some are not surrounded
by water all of the time.
        ISBN 0-516-20807-1 (lib. bdg.)   0-516-26366-8 (pbk.)
        1. Islands—Juvenile literature. [1. Islands.] I. Title. II. Series.
    GB471.F68   1998   97-17896
    551.42—dc21   CIP
                                                                          AC

How do you get to school? By bus? By car? Or do you walk? If you lived on an island too small to have its own school, you would have to take a boat!

3

An island is a piece of land with water all around it. You find islands in oceans, rivers, lakes, and bays.

The Statue of Liberty
stands on Liberty Island,
in Upper New York Bay.

Some islands are just big
enough to hold a few trees.

The largest islands are in oceans. How large can an island be?

If you look at a globe or a map of the world, the largest island seems to be Australia. But Australia is so huge that we call it a continent instead of an island.

The largest piece of land
called an island is Greenland.
Can you find Greenland on
a map?

Some countries, such as
Japan, are made up of islands.

The city of Venice, in Italy, is built on islands separated by canals.

Eight main islands, plus many islets (very small islands) make up the state of Hawaii. These islands are the tops of volcanic mountains that rose from the ocean floor ages ago.

A volcano is a big, deep crack in the earth. Hot, flowing rock, called lava, spouts out of the crack.

13

When lava cools and hardens,
it forms a mountain around
the volcano.

If the crack is in the ocean floor, the mountain around it may grow and grow until it rises above the water's surface. This is how some islands are formed.

Surtsey, an island near Iceland, was formed this way in 1963.

Islands are also created when water rises and covers land. Some parts of the land are too high for the water to cover, so they become islands.

The British Isles were formed that way. A long time ago they were connected to the continent of Europe. Then the sea level rose and cut them off, forming the islands.

Even today you can see something like that happening. Mont-Saint-Michel, in France, is an island when the ocean tide rises high.

When the tide flows out, you can walk or drive from the mainland to Mont-Saint-Michel.

Some islands were formed
by great sheets of ice,
called glaciers.

A glacier in Alaska

Much of the world was once covered by glaciers.

As they moved across the land, the glaciers piled up rocks and soil in front of them.

When the ice melted, some of those piles remained as islands. New York's Long Island is one of them.

Florida Keys

Islands often come in
groups or chains, like the
Thousand Islands and the
Florida Keys.

The Thousand Islands
lie in the St. Lawrence
River, between Canada
and the United States.
(There are really more
than 1,800 of them.)

The Thousand Islands

Coral islands are made of the rock-like skeletons of tiny sea animals.

Islands far from continents have their own kinds of plants and animals. The kiwi, for example, is a flightless bird found only in New Zealand.

Which kind of island would you like to live on? A green, sunny South Pacific island, with few people and a simple life?

Or New York City's
Manhattan Island, with tall
buildings and millions of
busy, busy people?

It might be nice to live
on one kind of island—
and visit another kind
on your vacation!

Words You Know

continent

island

Statue of Liberty

lava

volcano

coral

kiwi

canal

glacier

31

Index

About the Author

Allan Fowler is a freelance writer with a background in advertising. Born in New York, he now lives in Chicago and enjoys traveling.

Photo Credits

©: Larry Ulrich Photography: 14, 31 top left; NASA: 9; Photo Researchers: 5, 30 bottom right (Bill Bachmann); Photo Researchers: 27 (Rafael Macia), 17 (Maptec International Ltd./SPL), 25, 31 middle right (Tom McHugh), 22 (Porterfield/Chickering), 10 (Restec, Japan/SPL), 8, 30 top (WorldSat International/SS); Superstock, Inc.: 3, 6, 19, 23; Tony Stone Images: 13, 16, 31 top right (Paul Chesley), 11, 31 bottom left (David H. Endersbee), 19 inset (Sylvain Grandadam), 26 (Manfred Mehlig), 20, 31 bottom right (Bill Ross), cover (A & L Sinibaldi), 4 (Randy Wells), 7, 30 bottom left (Kim Westerskov), 24, 29, 31 middle left, (Stuart Westmorland).